THIS EMERGENCY JOKE K
BELONGS TO:

REAL NAME: ....

ALSO KNOWN AS: ....
....

IN AN EMERGENCY
YOU CAN CALL ME
ANYTHING YOU LIKE
SO LONG AS YOU DON'T
CALL ME LATE FOR
BREAKFAST!

HELP!

Illustrated by Judy Brown

PUFFIN BOOKS

PUFFIN BOOKS

Published by the Penguin Group
Penguin Books Ltd, 27 Wrights Lane, London W8 5TZ, England
Penguin Books USA Inc., 375 Hudson Street, New York, New York 10014, USA
Penguin Books Australia Ltd, Ringwood, Victoria, Australia
Penguin Books Canada Ltd, 10 Alcorn Avenue, Toronto, Ontario, Canada M4V 3B2
Penguin Books (NZ) Ltd, 182–190 Wairau Road, Auckland 10, New Zealand

Penguin Books Ltd, Registered Offices: Harmondsworth, Middlesex, England

First Published 1987
10 9

Copyright © Victoriana Ltd, 1987
Illustrations copyright © Judy Brown, 1987
All rights reserved

Typeset in Linotron Imprint by
Wyvern Typesetting, Bristol

Printed in Singapore by Imago Publishing Ltd.

Except in the United States of America, this book is sold subject
to the condition that it shall not, by way of trade or otherwise, be lent,
re-sold, hired out, or otherwise circulated without the publisher's
prior consent in any form of binding or cover other than that in which
it is published and without a similar condition including this condition
being imposed on the subsequent purchaser

WELCOME!

Whatever the emergency – you've broken your leg or a priceless vase, or both, you haven't done your homework, your gerbil's got the hiccups, the world has come to an end – DON'T WORRY! Equipped with this Emergency Joke Kit you can handle any situation. With the aid of these jokes you can cheer yourself, amuse your friends, sweet-talk your teachers, and fool your family *instantly*.

What's green, curved, and goes slam, slam, slam, slam?
A four-door cucumber.

Waiter, waiter, there are no cherries in this cherry cake!
Well, sir, would you expect to find dogs in a dog biscuit?

How do fleas like travelling?
They hop a dog.

What's worse than finding a maggot in your apple?
Finding half a maggot.

Why is a hippopotamus called a hippopotamus?
Because it looks like a hippopotamus, of course!

What children live in the sea?
Buoys.

Knock, knock.
Who's there?
Joe.
Joe who?
No Joe King!

What has five feet, three eyes and two tails?
A horse with spare parts!

Why did the girl push her friend under a steamroller?
Because she wanted a flatmate.

SALLY: Did you hear that the police are looking for a man with one eye called MacKenzie?
SIMON: *What's his other eye called?*

What's smaller than the mouth of an insect?
The food of an insect.

Doctor, I keep thinking I'm a pair of curtains.
Come on, now – pull yourself together!

What did the bar of chocolate say to the iced lolly?
Hi there, sucker.

What do you call a cat who has swallowed a duck?
A duck-filled fatty puss.

A young lad was helping his dad with do-it-yourself jobs around the house. 'You know, son,' said the father, 'you're just like lightning with that hammer.'

'Fast, eh?' said the boy.

'Oh, no – you never strike in the same place twice!'

What do you call a man with a spade on his head?
Doug.

And what do you call a man who hasn't got a spade on his head?
Douglas.

What sort of fish performs surgical operations?
A sturgeon.

What do you call a spy who hangs around in department stores?
A counter-spy.

How can you take five from one?
Every time you take five toes out of one sock.

Why did Robin Hood steal from the rich?
Because the poor had nothing worth taking.

SIMON: What are you going to be when you leave school?
SALLY: Old!

What do you call a monster who isn't pretty and isn't ugly?
Pretty ugly.

How did dinosaurs pass exams?
With extinction.

What does someone have to be to receive a state funeral?
Dead.

A river warden spotted a little boy fishing by a 'No Fishing' sign.
'Hey, can't you read?' he said. 'That sign says "No Fishing"!'
'But I'm not fishing,' said the little boy. 'I'm washing my bait!'

How does a Clever Dick spend hours on his homework every night, and yet get twelve hours' sleep?
He puts his homework underneath his mattress.

What's a grasshopper?
An insect on a pogo stick.

MOTHER: I thought I asked you to tell me when the kettle had boiled?
DAUGHTER: *You did. It boiled at 4.17.*

Did you hear about the meanest man in the world? He promised his sister a food mixer for her birthday – and gave her a wooden spoon!

Why did the nosey neighbours look over the garden fence?
Because they couldn't see through it.

How can you tell someone's a gossip?
They can lick an envelope after they've posted it.

TEACHER: In your exam you'll be allowed ten minutes for each question.
PUPIL: *How long are we allowed for the answer, Sir?*

POLLY: My boyfriend's got muscles like potatoes in his arms!
SALLY: *Yes, I've seen them – they're like mashed potatoes.*

I wish I had your picture –
Wouldn't it be nice!
I'd hang it in the cellar
To scare away the mice.

What do you get if you cross an unhappy man with a spaceship?
A moan rocket.

Why did the chicken cross the road?
To get to the other side.

Why did the elephant cross the road?
It was the chicken's day off.

Why did the rabbit cross the road?
To show his girlfriend that he'd got guts.

And why did the hedgehog cross the road?
To see his flatmates.

Which bird is always out of breath?
A puffin.

What do you get if you cross a galaxy with a toad?
Star warts.

On a coach trip to London a little girl kept sniffing.

'Haven't you got a hankie, dear?' asked a little old lady across the aisle.

'Yes,' replied the little girl. 'But I'm not supposed to talk to strangers, so I certainly can't lend you my hankie!'

What happened to the two blood cells?
They loved in vein.

How do we know New Zealand is a cold place?
Because the lamb they send over is always frozen!

PETER: Every time it rains I think of you.
PATTIE: *How romantic!*
PETER: Well, drip . . . drip . . . drip.

Knock, knock.
Who's there?
Felix.
Felix who?
Felix my ice cream again I'll hit him.

What's an ig?
An Eskimo house without a loo!

How can you tell that a theatre is sad?
Because all the seats are in tiers.

What coat has the most sleeves?
A coat of arms.

On which side does a chicken
have the most feathers?
On the outside.

Doctor, doctor, I've just
swallowed the film from my
camera.
Well, let's hope nothing develops.

*A ghoul stood on a bridge one
night,
Its lips were all a-quiver.
It gave a cough,
Its leg fell off
And floated down the river.*

Why are four-legged animals such bad dancers?
Because they have two left feet.

SALLY: I haven't shown you any of my holiday snaps!
SIMON: *No, and that's kind of you!*.

How can you tell a really crazy clock?
By its cuckoo.

What do you get if you pour hot water down a rabbit hole?
Hot cross bunnies.

What did the 'just married' spiders call their new home?
Newlywebs.

What musical instrument is best for sea-fishing?
A castanet.

Why did Batman climb a tree?
To look for Robin's nest.

PETER: I think my Mum wants me to leave home.
SIMON: *Why do you think that?*
PETER: She keeps wrapping my lunch in a road map.

What's another name for a sugar daddy?
A lollipop.

What do you call a man who makes faces all day?
A clockmaker.

SALLY: Did you know that in some countries they use fish instead of money?
SIMON: *They don't! Imagine the mess getting chocolate from a machine!*

What travels on land and on water and sucks up dirt?
A hoover-craft.

Doctor, doctor, my husband thinks he's a television.
Don't worry, I'll soon cure him of that.
But I don't want him cured – I just want him adjusted so that I can get Channel 4!

Did you hear about the idiot who took twenty-four hours to fill a salt cellar?
He pushed the salt through the little hole . . .

What happens when business is slow at a medicine factory?
You can hear a cough drop.

Why was the skeleton sad?
Because he'd been invited to a disco and had no body to go with.

What happened to the tailor who made his trousers from sun-blind material?
Every time the sun came out the trousers rolled down!

Why did the gnome wear
chocolate trousers?
*Because he wanted to be a
brownknee.*

PATTIE: I can do something
that no one else in the
world can.
PETER: *What's that?*
PATTIE: I can read my
handwriting.

Knock, knock.
Who's there?
Matthew.
Matthew who?
Matthew laces came undone.

When can you fall and be
unconscious, yet not be hurt?
When you fall asleep.

Why did the master baker close his shop?
Because the work was so crummy.

What is a dimple?
A pimple going the wrong way.

Why wouldn't the bus driver let the man stand on top of the bus?
Because it was a single decker.

Mummy, mummy, what are we having for dinner?
Shut up, son, and get back in the oven!

Did you hear the story of the three holes?
Well, well, well.

What did the scoutmaster say
when his car horn was fixed?
Beep repaired.

What is the most popular food served at a nudist camp?
Skinless-sausages!

What do you get if you cross a witch with an ice cube?
A cold spell.

Why do traffic wardens have yellow cuffs on their uniforms?
Because they don't carry handkerchiefs.

Knock, knock.
Who's there?
Closure.
Closure who?
Closure mouth when you're chewing.

Why does a baby pig eat so greedily?
To make a hog of himself.

LITTLE GHOST: Mum, can I go outside and play with Grandma?
MOTHER GHOST: *No, dear – you've dug her up twice already this week.*

'Your teeth are like the stars,' he said,
And pressed her hand so white.
He spoke the truth – for, like the stars,
Her teeth came out at night.

Did you hear about the farmer who became rich and famous?
He sold his story to the newspapers for cerealisation.

What's red, runs on wheels and
eats grass?
A bus – I lied about the grass.

What's the best way to get on TV?
Sit on it!

What do you get if you cross a
pigeon with a racing tip?
A bird that lays odds.

SIMON: I have to go to the
dentist about my
wisdom tooth.
SALLY: *Oh, are you having one
put in?*

What's the difference between a
square peg in a round hole and a
kilo of lard?
*One's a fat lot of good and the
other's a good lot of fat!*

Why did the man go out and buy a set of tools?
Because everyone kept telling him he had a screw loose.

Why is an old loaf of bread like a mouse diving into its hole?
Because you can see it's stale.

A giraffe went into a fast-food restaurant, and asked for a hamburger with cheese. He sat down at a table, ate his hamburger, and then got up to pay. 'That'll be £5.25, please,' said the cashier, 'and thank you for choosing this restaurant, we don't see many giraffes in here.'

'At your prices, I'm not surprised!' said the giraffe.

Knock, knock.
Who's there?
Farmer.
Farmer who?
Farmer birthday I'm getting a
new watch.

What's yellow and flickers?
A lemon with a loose connection.

Why do golfers wear two pairs of
trousers?
In case they get a hole in one.

Which hand should you use to stir your tea?
Neither – you should use a spoon!

Doctor, doctor, my wife thinks she's a duck.
You better bring her in to see me straight away.
I can't do that – she's already flown south for the winter.

PATTIE: I don't believe that rabbits' feet are lucky.
PETER: *Why not?*
PATTIE: Well, they're not very lucky for the rabbits, are they!

Why are telephone wires so high up in the air?
To keep up the conversation!

What do you call a flying dog?
A Skye terrier.

Mary had a little lamb,
You've heard this tale before.
But did you know
She passed her plate
And had a little more?

PATTIE: Do you think ghosts
        like being dead?
PETER: Of corpse they do!

What's the difference between
snow and Sunday?
*Snow can fall on any day of the
week.*

What do men do standing up,
women do sitting down, and dogs
do on three legs?
Shake hands!

TEACHER:	I have all your surnames, but I'd like you to give me your first names, please.
PUPIL:	*My name's Arthur Micky Brown.*
TEACHER:	Thank you. I'll call you Arthur Brown.
PUPIL:	*My Dad won't like that, Miss!*
TEACHER:	Why not?
PUPIL:	*Because he doesn't like people taking the Micky out of me.*

What's a skeleton's favourite musical instrument?
A trombone.

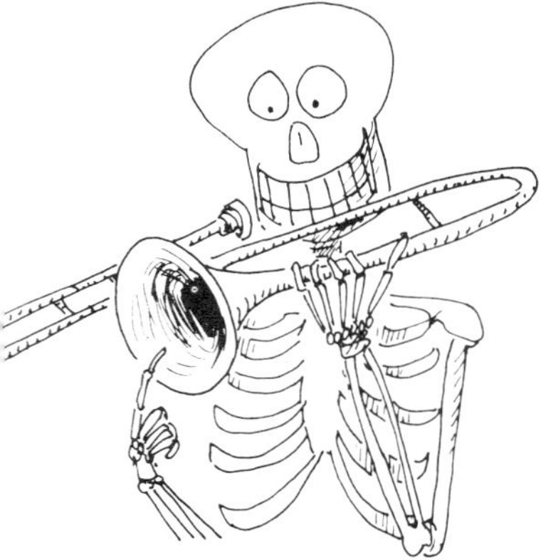

What do you get if you cross a
frog with a decathlete?
*Someone who pole vaults without
a pole.*

Where do Five Star like to go on
holiday?
The Milky Way.

SALLY: I fell over twenty feet
last night.
SIMON: *Did you hurt yourself?*
SALLY: No, I was just trying to
get out of the cinema.

What sort of motorbike can cook eggs?
A scrambler.

What's French, very tall, and wobbles?
The Trifle Tower.

SIMON: Why do traffic lights turn red?
SALLY: *I don't know – why do traffic lights turn red?*
SIMON: Wouldn't you – if you had to stop and go in the middle of the road?

Did you hear about the schoolgirl who described rhubarb as celery with high blood pressure?

What did the doctor advise the
sick snooker player?
To get more greens.

Why is the Prince of Wales like cloudy weather?
Because he's likely to reign.

Why does Bob Geldof wear red, white and blue braces?
To keep his trousers up.

What do you call two chemist shops?
A pair of Boots.

What was the name of the first-ever underwater spy?
James Pond.

Which vegetable goes best with jacket potatoes?
Button mushrooms.

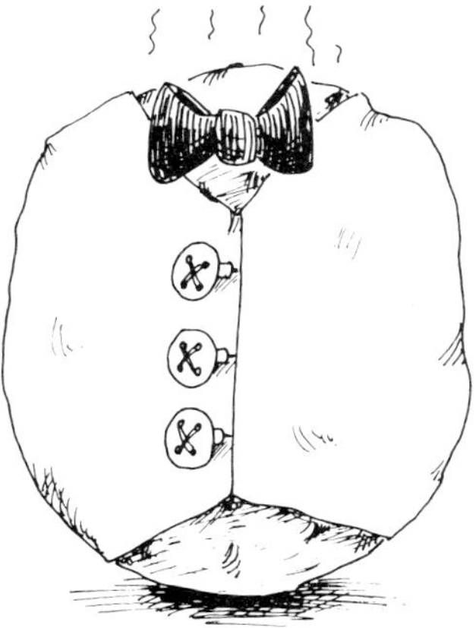

PATTIE: My new boyfriend's got a hobby he really sticks to.
SALLY: *What's that?*
PATTIE: He sits glued to EastEnders every night.

Two men were waiting in a doctor's surgery, and got talking.
 'I'm aching from arthritis,' said one.
 'Pleased to meet you,' said the other. 'I'm Basil from Birmingham.'

PETER: I think your sister's really spoiled.
SIMON: *No, that's just her perfume.*